10 EASY LESSONS

TEACH YOURSELF

CLASS...
GUIT...

b...

Brett D...

 MUSIC EXCHANGE (Manchest...

For more information on the *10 Easy Lessons, Teach Yourself Play* series contact;

Music Exchange
Claverton Road, Manchester
M23 9ZA, England
Ph: (0161) 946 1234
Fax: (0161) 946 1195

www.music-exchange.co.uk

Contents

Introduction .... Page 3
Approach to Practice 3
Parts of the Classical Guitar 4
Guitar Preparation 5
Tuning 6
Fretboard Diagrams 7
Reading Guitar Music 8
Rhythm 9
Playing Position 10
Left and Right Hand Technique 11

LESSON 1 .... Page 12
Picking the Strings 12
The Rest Stroke 12
Notes on the First String 13
Alternating Fingers 13
The Repeat Sign 14
Notes on the Second String 16
Notes on the Third String 18

LESSON 2 .... Page 19
Rests 19
Aura Lee 19
Yankee Doodle 20
In the Light of the Moon 20
Good King Wenceslas 20

LESSON 3 .... Page 21
Notes on the Fourth String 21
Picking with the Thumb 21
Using the Right Hand Thumb
    and Fingers Together 22
The Three Four Time Signature 23
The Dotted Half Note 23
The Tie 23

LESSON 4 .... Page 24
Classical Guitar Music Notated
    in Two Parts 24
Notes on the Fifth String 25
Notes on the Sixth String 26
The Major Scale 28
The Octave 28
The C Major Scale 28

LESSON 5 .... Page 29
The Eighth Note 29
Skip to My Lou 29
The Galway Piper 29
The Eighth Rest 30
The 1812 Overture 30
The Lead-In 30
First and Second Endings 30
The William Tell Overture 30

LESSON 6 .... Page 31
Sharp Signs 31
The G Major Scale 31
Key Signatures 32
Duets 32
Minuet in G 32
The Natural Sign 33
Minuet in Em 33

LESSON 7 .... Page 34
The Free Stroke 34
Malaguena 35
Asturias 35
Chords, Arpeggios 36
Picking Two Notes Together 37
Picking Three Notes Together 37
Picking Four Notes Together 37

LESSON 8 .... Page 38
Classical Guitar Pieces 38
Waltz 38
Andantino (Carcassi) 40
Andantino (Giuliani) 40
Waltz 41
Study in Am 41
Flat Signs 42
Study in C 42

LESSON 9 .... Page 43
The Dotted Quarter Note 43
Andante 43
Minuet 44
The Six Eight Time Signature 45
Barcarolle 45
The Eighth Note Triplet 46
Allegretto 46

LESSON 10 .... Page 47
The Half Bar 47
The Full Bar 48
Study in C Major 48
Dynamics 49
Allegro 49
The Sixteenth Note, The Sixteenth Rest 50
Study in A Minor 50
Using the Rest and Free Stroke Together 51
Study in E Minor 51

How to Tune Your Guitar .... Page 54
Scales, Natural Notes, Chromatic Scale 54
The Major Scale 55
The Minor Scale 56
Keys and Key Signatures 57
Relative Keys 58
Glossary of Musical Terms 59

Introduction

10 EASY LESSONS CLASSICAL GUITAR has been designed to be used by people who would like to learn to play Classical guitar. It is suitable either for someone who has no previous knowledge of the guitar or guitar players who are experienced in other styles.

This book will introduce you to the basic fundamentals of Classical Guitar. It covers all the important techniques that uniquely apply to this style. The opening section which deals with Reading Music, Rhythm, Playing Position and left and right hand technique will prepare you for your first lesson.

In the first two lessons you will learn the notes on the first three strings and your first basic single note melodies. At this stage you will be using only the fingers off the right hand.

Lesson 3 introduces the notes on the fourth string and the use of the right hand thumb. By the completion of lesson 4 you will be playing some interesting sounding exercises that combine the use of both the right hand thumb and fingers. You will also learn your first scale.

Lessons 5 and 6 further your theory by introducing things such as eighth notes, the sharp sign, the natural sign and key signatures. Duets are also featured in lesson 6.

Lessons 7 and 8 introduce the free stroke and picking several notes at once. You will also learn your first complete Classical guitar pieces, written by famous Classical guitar composers.

The final lessons cover more techniques, note values and dynamics. By the end of lesson 10 you will learn many more interesting Classical guitar pieces.

A special section at the end of the book has been included. In this section tuning, scales, keys, key signatures and relative keys are discussed. A glossary of musical terms is also included.

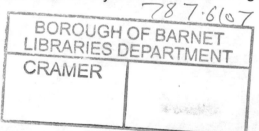

Approach to Practice

From the beginning you should set yourself a goal. Many people learn guitar because of a desire to play like their favourite artist, or to play a certain style of music (e.g. Classical, Jazz etc.). Motivations such as these will help you to persevere through the more difficult sections of work. As you develop it will be important to adjust and update your goals.

It is important to have a correct approach to practice. You will benefit more from several short practices (e.g. 15-30 minutes per day) than one or two long sessions per week. This is especially so in the early stages, because of the basic nature of the material being studied. In a practice session you should divide your time evenly between the study of new material and the revision of past work. It is a common mistake for semi-advanced students to practice only the pieces they can already play well. Although this is more enjoyable, it is not a very satisfactory method of practice. You should also try to correct mistakes and experiment with new ideas.

It is the author's belief that the guidance of an experienced teacher will be an invaluable aid in your progress.

Parts of the Classical Guitar

The **classical** guitar has nylon strings and a wider neck than the other types of guitar. It is most commonly used for playing Classical, Flamenco and Fingerstyles. Generally it is much cheaper than other types of guitar and is recommended for beginning guitarists.

The Classical Guitar

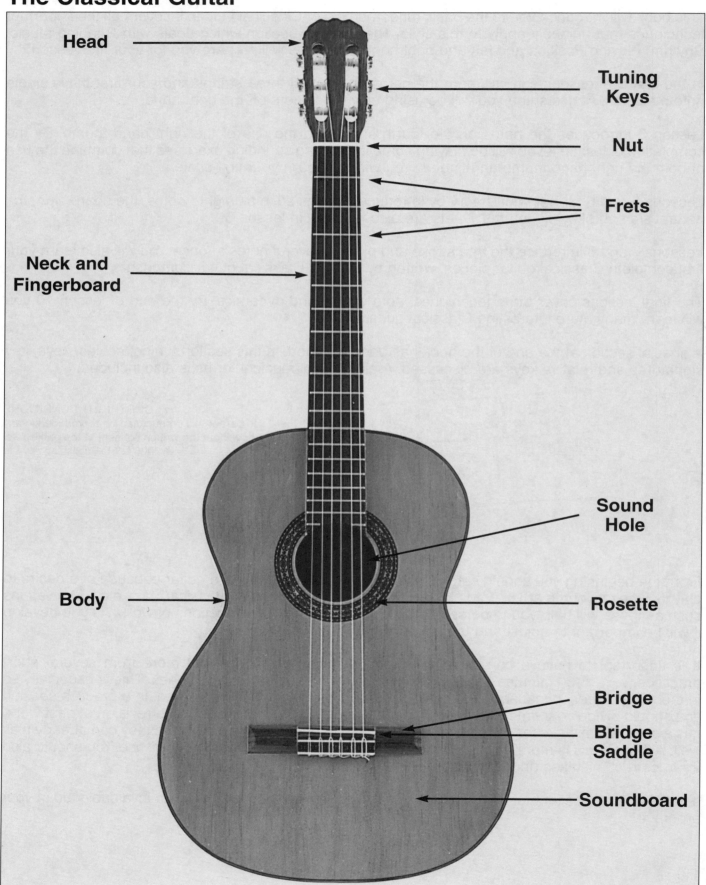

Head

Tuning Keys

Nut

Frets

Neck and Fingerboard

Sound Hole

Body

Rosette

Bridge

Bridge Saddle

Soundboard

Guitar Preparation

Strings

It is important to have the correct set of strings fitted to your guitar, especially if you are a beginner. Until you build enough strength in your hands to fret the chords cleanly, light gauge or low tension strings are recommended. A reputable music store which sells guitar strings should be able to assist with this. Do not put steel strings on a classical guitar or it will damage the neck of the guitar.

Fitting the Strings

Strings must be correctly fitted to the guitar otherwise you will encounter tuning problems. In the early stages of learning the guitar it is recommended that you get a qualified guitar repairer or an experienced guitar player to fit the strings to your guitar.

Tying the string to the bridge: There are basically two methods to tying the string to the bridge. Study the following diagrams. With both types of knot shown it is important to finish the knot behind the back of the bridge. This will reduce the possibility of the string slipping.

Option 1.

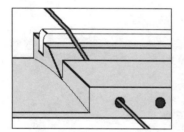 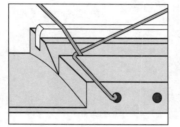 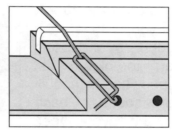

Option 2.

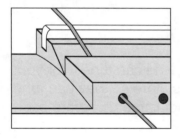 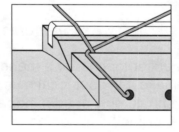 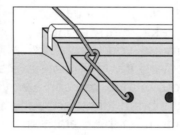 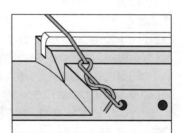

Tying the string to the tuning key: It is important to have a short length of the string protruding through the hole in the tuning key barrel. This part of the string can then be clamped to the barrel as the string is coiled onto the barrel. See the adjacent diagram. The string should coil neatly around the barrel at least 4 -5 times.

String Height

The height of the strings from the fretboard (sometimes called the 'action') is very important to the feel of the guitar. If the strings are set too high, it will be more difficult to push the strings onto the fretboard. If the strings are set too low, the strings will rattle against the fretboard causing a buzzing noise. The height of the strings is determined by two things, the nut and the bridge saddle. These adjustments should be carried out by a qualified guitar repairer.

Tuning

Tuning Your Guitar to the CD

Before you commence each lesson or practice session you will need to tune your guitar. If your guitar is out of tune everything you play will sound incorrect even though you are holding the correct notes. On the accompanying CD the **first six tracks** correspond to the **six strings of the guitar**. For a complete description of how to tune your guitar, see page 52.

 1. 6th String
E Note (Thickest string)

 2. 5th String
A Note

 3. 4th String
D Note

 4. 3rd String
G Note

 5. 2nd String
B Note

 6. 1st String
E Note (Thinnest string)

Electronic Tuner

The easiest and most accurate way to tune your guitar is by using an **electronic tuner**. An electronic tuner allows you to tune each string individually to the tuner, by indicating whether the notes are sharp (too high) or flat (too low). The electronic tuner has an inbuilt microphone to pick up the sound of each string as it is plucked. There are several types of electronic guitar tuners but most are relatively inexpensive and simple to operate. Tuning using other methods is difficult for beginning guitarists and it takes many months to master, so we recommend you purchase

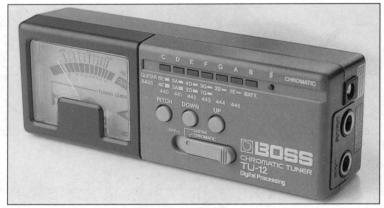
Electronic Tuner

an electronic tuner, particularly if you do not have a guitar teacher or a friend who can tune it for you. Also if your guitar is way out of tune you can always take it to your local music store so they can tune it for you. Once a guitar has been tuned correctly it should only need minor adjustments before each practice session. To learn to tune the guitar using other methods see page 52.

Using the Compact Disc

It is recommended that you have a copy of the accompanying compact disc that includes all the examples in this book. The book shows you where to put your fingers and what technique to use and the recording lets you hear how each example should sound. Practice the examples slowly at first, gradually increasing tempo. Once you are confident you can play the example evenly without stopping the beat, try playing along with the recording. You will hear a drum beat at the beginning of each example, to lead you into the example and to help you keep time. To play along with the CD your guitar must be in tune with it (see above). If you have tuned using an electronic tuner (see above) your guitar will already be in tune with the CD. A small diagram of a compact disc with a number as shown below indicates a recorded example.

12. ← CD Track Number

Fretboard Diagrams

Fretboard diagrams are used throughout this book to show you where to place your left hand fingers. A fretboard diagram is a grid of horizontal and vertical lines representing the strings and frets of the guitar as shown below.

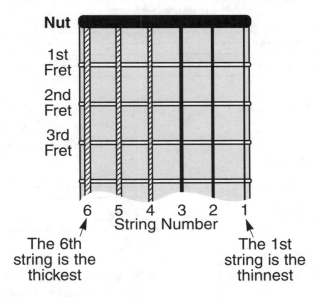

An open circle shown above the nut indicates an open string, i.e. the string is played 'open' without the need of holding down the string at a particular fret. The diagram below shows the first string open, the note E.

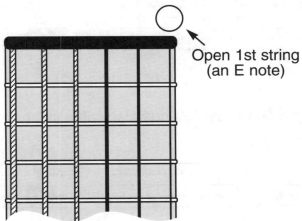

Open 1st string
(an E note)

A black circle drawn on a string indicates a fretted note. The number inside the circle refers to which left hand finger is used to play that note. The diagram below highlights the note on the first fret of the first string (an F note), to be played with the first finger.

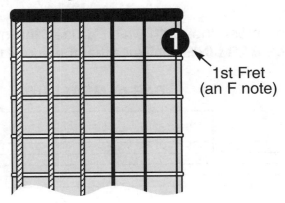

1st Fret
(an F note)

Reading Guitar Music

The musical alphabet consists of 7 letters: **A B C D E F G**

Music is written on a **STAFF**, which consists of 5 parallel lines between which there are 4 spaces.

MUSIC STAFF

THE TREBLE OR 'G' CLEF is placed at the beginning of each staff line.

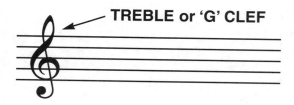

The other lines and spaces on the staff are named as such:

This clef indicates the position of the note G with the centre of the clef being written on the second staff line (a G note).

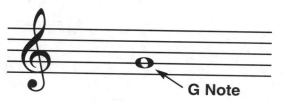

Extra notes can be added by the use of short lines, called **LEGER LINES**.

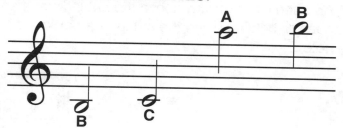

When a note is placed on the staff its head indicates its position, e.g.:

This is a G NOTE

This is a C NOTE

When the note head is below the middle staff line the stem points upward and when the head is above the middle line the stem points downward. A note placed on the middle line (**B**) can have its stem pointing either up or down.

BAR LINES are drawn across the staff, which divides the music into sections called **BARS** or **MEASURES**. A **DOUBLE BAR LINE** signifies either the end of the music, or the end of an important section of it.

BAR or MEASURE

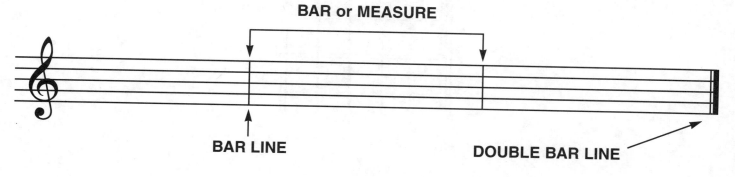

BAR LINE

DOUBLE BAR LINE

Rhythm

Music notes are always played to a strict rhythm or beat. The first thing to understand about rhythm is how many beats are in each measure or bar of music.

Time Signatures

At the beginning of each piece of music, after the treble clef, is the **TIME SIGNATURE**.

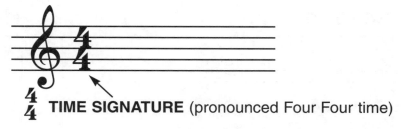

TIME SIGNATURE (pronounced Four Four time)

The time signature indicates the number of beats per bar (the top number) and the type of note receiving one beat (the bottom number). For example:

4 – this indicates 4 beats per bar.

4 – this indicates that each beat is worth a quarter note (see below).

In each bar of music below there is four beats.

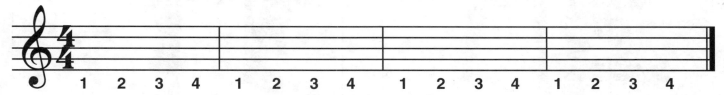

The next thing to understand about rhythm is the length or value of each note. When a note is written as an open circle only it is called a **whole note** and lasts for a total of four beats.

 This is a whole note.
It lasts for four beats.

A whole note lasts for one entire bar of ₄ time. In the following piece of music a whole note is played on the first beat of each bar and held for four beats. The sound of the note should ring for four beats. The big counting number **1** below the music indicates the note is played. The smaller numbers 2 3 4 indicate the note is held until the next note.

The other two common note values are the **half** and **quarter** notes.

This is a half note.
It lasts for two beats.

This is a quarter note.
It lasts for one beats.

There are two half notes or four quarter notes to each bar of ₄ time.

Playing Position

It is essential that correct playing position is used when playing the guitar. The basics of guitar technique include seating, holding the instrument and the correct position of both hands.

Seating

Sit towards the front edge of a chair with your left leg raised. An adjustable guitar footstool is recommended which can be purchased at most music stores. Experiment with the height of the footstool and the height of the chair until you reach a seating position you feel comfortable with.

Holding the Guitar

The guitar is secured at four points of the body. The left and right thighs, the forearm and the chest. The guitar should rest flat on your left thigh and not lean backwards. Angle the guitar slightly upwards as shown in the photo above.

Right Arm Position

The right forearm is positioned over the body of the guitar so that the right hand is in position to pluck the strings. The elbow should not extend out to the front of the guitar. The angle of the right hand is such that the knuckles should virtually be in line with the direction of the strings.

Left Arm Position

If your seating position is comfortable and you are securing the guitar correctly then your left arm will easily reach the first four frets of the guitar. Your left arm should not be close to your body nor be pushing away from your body. It should be able to move freely up and down the entire fretboard.

Left and Right Hand Technique

Left Hand Fingers

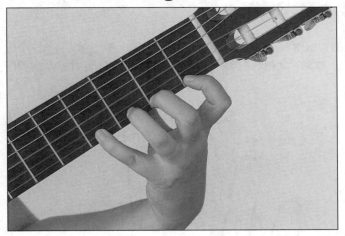

The fingers of the left hand should be slightly arched. You must be able to spread the fingers across the first four frets, using the fingertips only to hold down the string, just behind the fretwire.

Left Hand Thumb

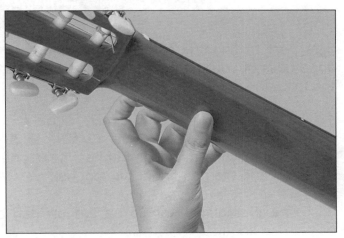

The thumb must be behind the neck at all times and never reach over the top of the neck. It should be at a slight angle and approximately in line with the second finger of your left hand hand.

Right Hand Fingers

The right hand fingers should be slightly curved and positioned as close as possible to the first three strings. The wrist should be slightly arched with a slight twist downwards. See photo below.

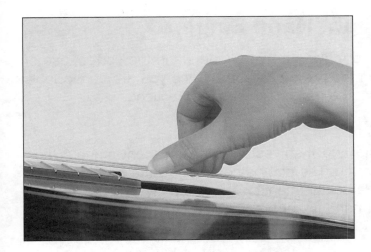

The left hand fingers are numbered as such.

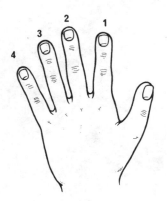

Right Hand Thumb

The right hand thumb should make contact with the bass strings slightly further along the strings than the fingers. The photo below is the view of the guitarist and shows the correct angle for the thumb in relation to the strings

The letters *p*, *i*, *m* and *a* are used to indicate the right hand fingers.

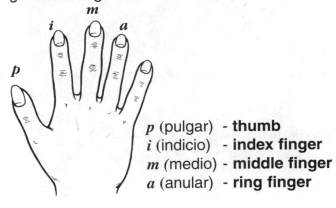

p (pulgar) - **thumb**
i (indicio) - **index finger**
m (medio) - **middle finger**
a (anular) - **ring finger**

Lesson 1

Picking the Strings

It is best to fingerpick the strings with your **fingernails** as this gives a better sound. Let the fingernails of your right hand grow to a length that is comfortable for your playing with attention to the following points.

1. The length of the nail should be approximately 2 - 3mm (3/32 - 5/32"). Generally the middle finger has the shortest nail and the ring finger the longest.

2. The thumb nail should be longer than all three fingers.

3. Fingernails should be shaped using a nail file (emery board) so that they have a rounded edge and flow smoothly off the string after it has been picked.

4. Experiment with the overall shape of each nail. You may find having a fingernail longer on one side of the finger helpful with picking a string cleanly.

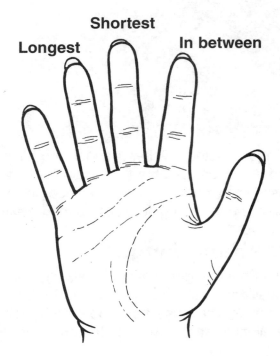

Picking With Your Right Hand Fingers

Before trying to pick the strings with your right hand make sure you understand the correct use of right hand technique. Study the text and photos on the previous pages. Once you are comfortably seated with the right arm and right hand in position, the rest stroke can be practiced.

The Rest Stroke

The rest stroke is when the finger picks the string and then rests on the adjacent string. When executed correctly it produces a strong clear full sound. The photos below show the position of the first finger, before and after picking the first string. Particular attention should be given to the position and shape of the right hand finger. Notice the right hand finger braced on a bass string.

Position first finger to pick first string.

First finger rests on second string after picking first string

Notes on the First String *(E)*

The first notes to learn are the notes E, F and G on the first string.

E Note *(1st string)*

The open first string is an E note.

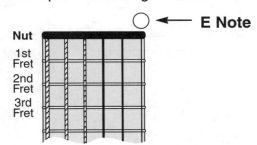

This E note is written in the fourth space of the staff.

The first exercise is four bars long. The note E is played on the first beat of each bar. Each E note is a whole note, therefore it lasts for the duration of the entire bar (4 beats).

Alternating Fingers

You must alternate your *i* (index) and *m* (middle) fingers when playing single melody lines. In the following exercise the *i* finger plays the E note in the 1st and 3rd bars, the *m* finger plays the E note in the 2nd and 4th bars.

After the first E note is played the *i* finger should rest on the second string until the *m* finger is ready to pick the E note in the second bar. The *i* finger should move from the second string at the same time the *m* finger picks the E note, which then comes to rest on the second string until the *i* finger is ready to play the E note in the third bar, and so on.

The fingers should give the impression of 'walking' across the string.

 ## 7. Whole Note Exercise

The next exercise is also four bars long except half notes are used. The E note is played on the 1st and 3rd beats of each bar. Remember to alternate between your *i* and *m* fingers.

 ## 8. Half Note Exercise

Quarter notes are used in the next exercise. A note is played on each beat of the bar. With this exercise you should particularly feel the 'walking' movement with the alternating fingers.

9. Quarter Note Exercise

F Note *(1st string)*

The note on the first fret of the first string is an F note. Use the first finger of your left hand to fret this note.

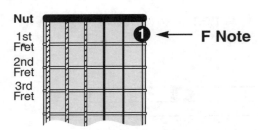

This F note is written on the top line of the staff.

The next exercise features the F note and uses both whole notes and half notes.

10.

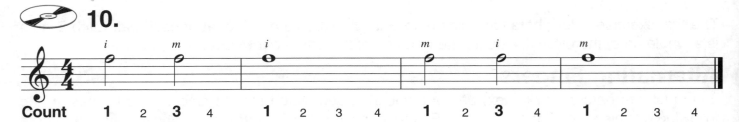

G Note *(1st string)*

The note on the third fret of the first string is a G note. Use the third finger of your left hand to fret this note.

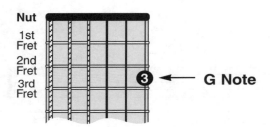

This G note is written above the top line of the staff.

The Repeat Sign

The two dots at the end of the staff before the double bar lines are called a **repeat sign** and mean that you play the exercise again from the start. This exercise is eight bars long and contains whole, half and quarter notes.

Note: The small numbers written below the staff are measure or bar numbers.

11.

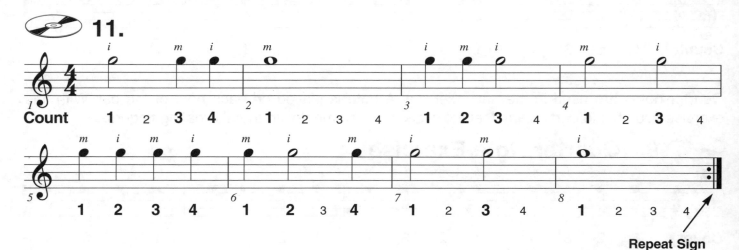

Repeat Sign

Combining the Notes E, F and G

In each of the previous exercises only one note was used. The following exercises combine the notes E, F and G. This will require a little more co-ordination as both the left and right hand fingers will be changing.

Left Hand Position - Review

Before trying the next exercise review the position of your left hand. Make sure your left hand fingers are evenly spread across the first four frets. The fingers should hover just above each fret.

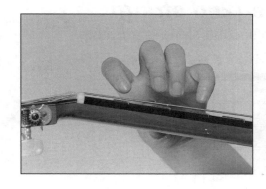

Check your left hand technique

Notes on the Second String (B)

There are three notes to learn on the second string, the open B note, the C note on the first fret and the D note on the third fret.

B Note *(2nd string)*

The open second string is a B note.

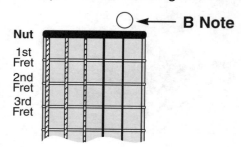

This B note is written on the middle line of the staff.

Exercise 16 introduces the open B note.
It is good practice to reverse the order of your right hand alternating fingers as shown in the following exercise. Practice all the following exercises and melodies both ways.

16.

C Note *(2nd string)*

The note on the first fret of the second string is a C note. Use the first finger of your left hand to fret this note.

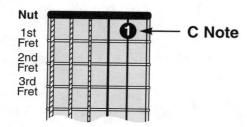

This C note is written in the third space of the staff.

Exercise 17 introduces the C note on the second string.

17.

D Note *(2nd string)*

The note on the third fret of the second string is an F note. Use the third finger of your left hand to fret this note.

This D note is written on the fourth line of the staff.

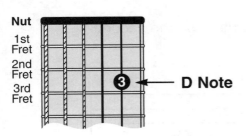

Exercise 18 introduces the D note on the second string.

18.

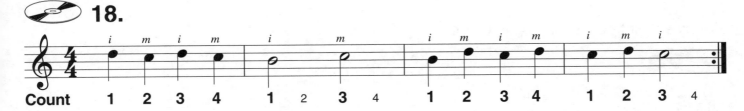

Summary - The Notes So Far

You have now learnt six notes on the first two strings. When changing between two strings use minimal movement with the right hand fingers. Practice the following exercise until you can feel a smooth transition between both strings

19.

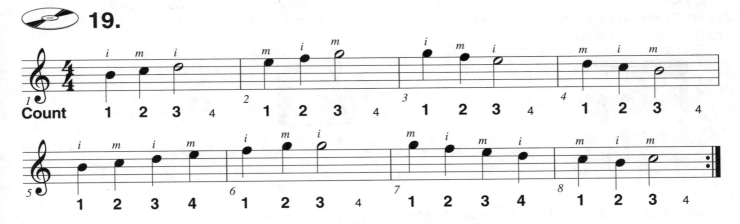

As you learn more notes you will be able to develop a repertoire of well known songs as well as a selection of popular Classical guitar pieces. The following exercise is a simple variation of a popular melody that can be played with knowing only a small number of notes.

20. Ode to Joy

Notes on the Third String *(G)*

There are two notes to learn on the third string, the open G note and the A note on the second fret.

G Note *(3rd string)*

The open third string is a G note.

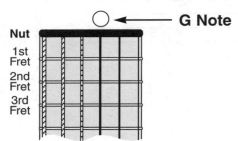

This G note is written on the second line of the staff.

Exercise 21 introduces the open G note.

21.

A Note *(3rd string)*

The note on the second fret of the third string is an A note. Use the second finger of your left hand to fret this note.

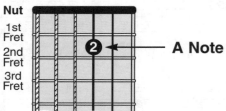

This A note is written in the second space of the staff.

Exercise 22 introduces the A note on the third string.

22.

You now know eight notes on the first three strings.

23.

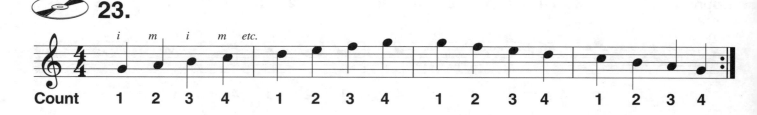

Lesson 2

Rests

A **rest** is a period of silence. **Small** count-numbers are placed under rests.

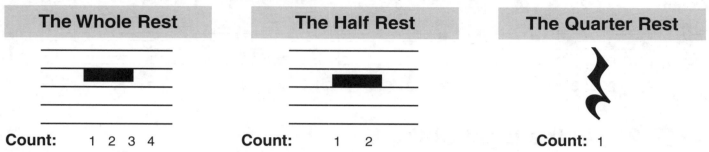

The Whole Rest	The Half Rest	The Quarter Rest
Count: 1 2 3 4	**Count:** 1 2	**Count:** 1

This is a **whole rest**.
It indicates one bar of silence.
A whole rest in $\frac{4}{4}$ time indicates
four beats of silence.

This is a **half rest**.
It indicates two beats of silence.

This is a **quarter rest**.
It indicates one beat of silence.

Each type of rest is demonstrated in the following exercise. If a rest comes after you have played a note, you must stop the note sounding. To do this, lift your finger off the fret but keep it lightly touching the string (bars 1, 3 and 8). To stop an open string sounding, lightly touch it with any finger of your left hand (bars 2, 4 and 6. Listen to the recording to hear the correct effect of the rest.

24.

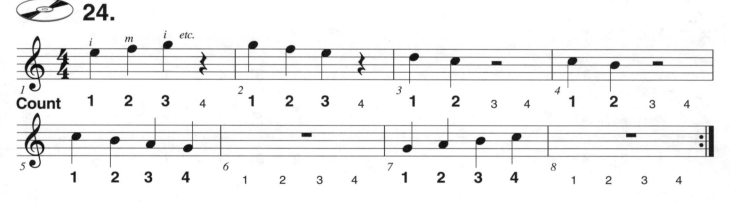

The following melody contains rests.

25. Aura Lee

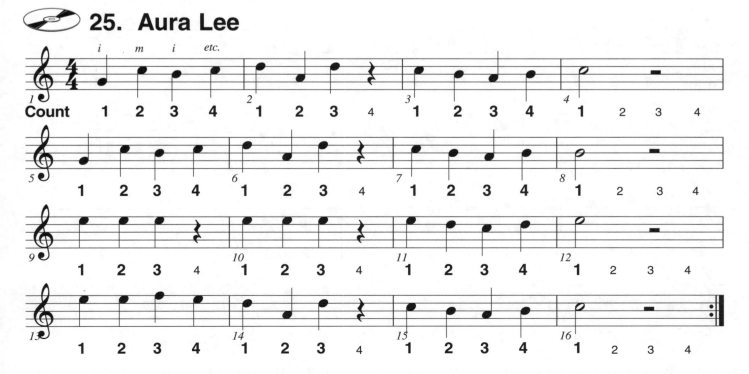

20

The following pieces use all the notes on the first three strings.

26. Yankee Doodle

27. In the Light of the Moon

28. Good King Wenceslas

Lesson 3

Notes on the Fourth String *(D)*

There are three notes to learn on the fourth string, the open D note, the E note on the second fret and the F note on the third fret.

D Note *(4th string)*

The open fourth string is a D note.

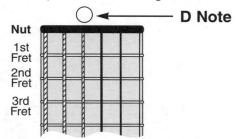

This D note is written in the space below the staff.

Picking with the Thumb (*p*)

The 4th, 5th and 6th strings are picked with the thumb (*p*). In almost all cases a free stroke is used. After striking each D note in the following exercise the thumb should move over the third string and return to its original position ready to strike the D note again. Your thumb should feel as if it is moving in small circles.

The thumb should move over the 3rd string after picking the 4th string.

29.

Count   1   2   3   4   1   2   3   4   1   2   3   4   1   2   3   4

E Note *(4th string)*

The note on the second fret of the fourth string is an E note. Use the second finger of your left hand to fret this note.

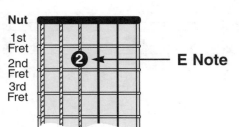

This E note is written on the first line of the staff.

30.

Count   1   2   3   4   1   2   3   4   1   2   3   4   1   2   3   4

F Note *(4th string)*

The note on the third fret of the fourth string is an F note. Use the third finger of your left hand to fret this note.

This F note is written in the first space of the staff.

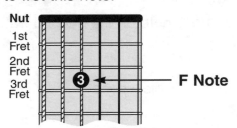

31.

Using the Right Hand Thumb and Fingers Together

You may encounter problems at first when playing a melody that uses both the bass and treble strings because you will be using a rest stroke on the first three strings and a free stroke on the bass strings. This may feel a little uncomfortable at first, especially when notes on the fourth and third string follow each other.

The next exercise uses the open fourth and third strings only. Before playing this exercise make sure your right hand is in the correct position. Keep your right hand steady and do not alter the shape of the hand as you change from picking with the fingers and the thumb.

Special attention should be given to the suggested right hand fingering.

32.

Now try an exercise that uses all the notes on the fourth and third strings.

33.

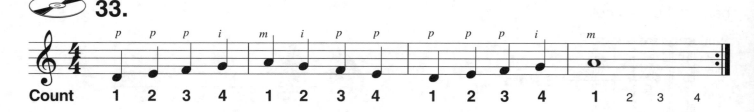

Exercise 34 highlights all the notes studied so far.

34.

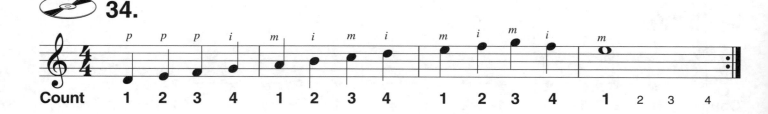

The Three Four Time Signature

This time signature is called the **three four time signature**. It indicates there are **three** beats in each bar. Three four time is also known as waltz time. There are three quarter notes in one bar of $\frac{3}{4}$ time.

The following exercise is in three four time. Listen to the recording to hear the correct rhythm.

 **35.**

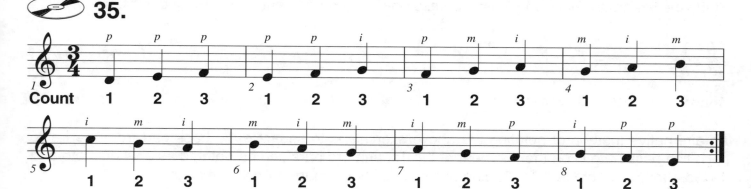

The Dotted Half Note

Count: 1 2 3

A dot placed after a note or strum extends its value by **half**. A dot placed after a half note or half note strum means that you hold it for three beats. One dotted half note makes one bar of music in $\frac{3}{4}$ time. There is one dotted half note strum in one bar of music in $\frac{3}{4}$ time.

The dotted half note is used throughout the following exercise.

36.

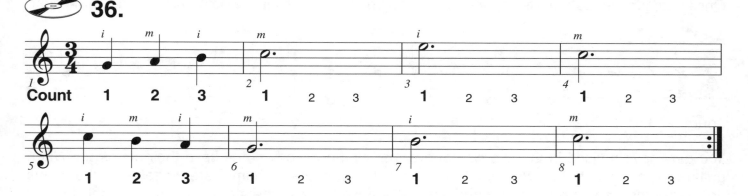

The Tie

A **tie** is a curved line that connects two notes with the **same** position on the staff. A tie tells you to pick the **first** note only, and to hold it for the length of both notes.

Count: 1   2   3   1   2   3

Pick the D note and hold it for six counts.

Lesson 4

Classical Guitar Music Notated in Two Parts

Classical guitar music is often notated in two separate parts. The purpose of this is to clearly see each 'voice' or 'part' of the music. This mainly is used to show the separation of the bass part (played with the right hand thumb) and the treble part (played with the right hand fingers).

Study the example below which uses a bass note on the first beat of the 1st and 3rd bars.

An alternative method of notating the above exercise is to separate the bass part from the treble part. The bass note D on the first beat of the 1st and 3rd bars can be notated as a whole note and tied to another D note in the following bar. This is shown in the following example.

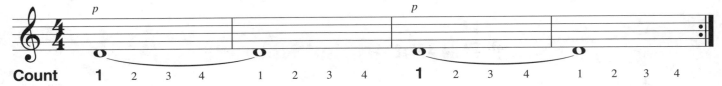

The treble part can also be notated by placing a rest on the first beat of the 1st and 3rd bars.

Once you can see both parts separately it is then possible to visualize both parts on the same staff.

37.

You may have noticed in the exercise above that all the melody notes have their stems up. When guitar music is notated in two parts, the bass notes (right hand thumb) are written with the stems down and the treble notes (right hand fingers) are written with the stems up. This is highlighted in the following exercise.

38.

Notes on the Fifth String *(A)*

There are three notes to learn on the fifth string, the open A note, the B note on the second fret and the C note on the third fret.

A Note *(5th string)*

The open fifth string is an A note.

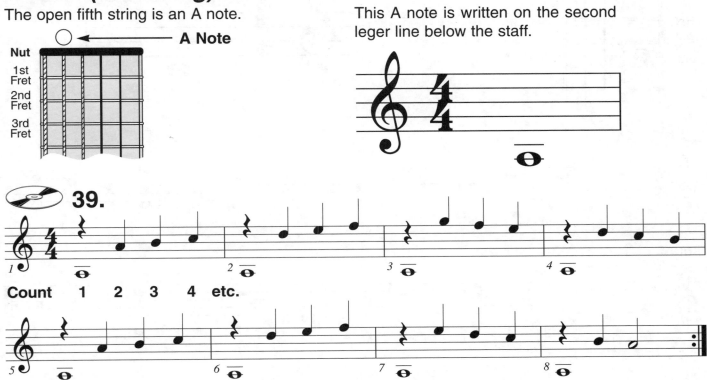

This A note is written on the second leger line below the staff.

39.

Count 1 2 3 4 etc.

B Note *(5th string)*

The note on the second fret of the fifth string is a B note. Use the second finger of your left hand to fret this note.

This B note is written under the first leger line below the staff.

Special attention snould be given to the left hand fingering in bar numbers 5 and 6. It is important to hold the B note on the last beat of bar 5 for the entire duration of bar 6. You will therefore need to use the 4th finger of your left hand to finger the G note in bar 6.

40.

Count 1 2 3 4 etc.

Hold

C Note (5th string)

The note on the third fret of the fifth string is a C note. Use the third finger of your left hand to fret this note.

This C note is written on the first leger line below the staff.

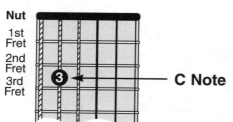

41.

Count   1   2   3   4   etc.

Notes on the Sixth String (E)

There are three notes to learn on the sixth string, the open E note, the F note on the first fret and the G note on the third fret.

E Note (6th string)

The open sixth string is an E note.

This E note is written under the third leger line below the staff.

42.

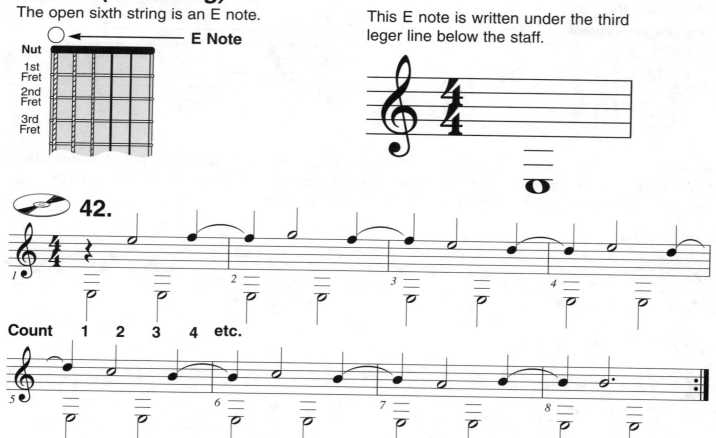

Count   1   2   3   4   etc.

F Note *(6th string)*

The note on the first fret of the sixth string is an F note. Use the first finger of your left hand to fret this note.

This F note is written on the third leger line below the staff.

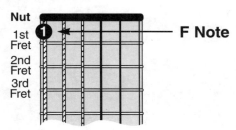

G Note *(6th string)*

The note on the third fret of the sixth string is a G note. Use the third finger of your left hand to fret this note.

This G note is written under the second leger line below the staff.

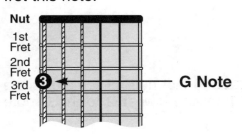

Left Hand Technique

At this stage it will be necessary to review your left hand technique. The notes on the sixth string can be difficult to reach comfortably at first, particularly the F note on the first fret. Make sure your left hand is correctly in position with the thumb behind the neck and your fingers arched evenly across the first four frets.

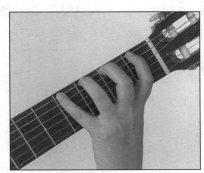

Left hand technique is essential when reaching for the notes on the 6th string.

The following exercise features notes on the sixth and fifth strings. An open 1st string is played after each bass note. Remember to use alternating fingers.

43.

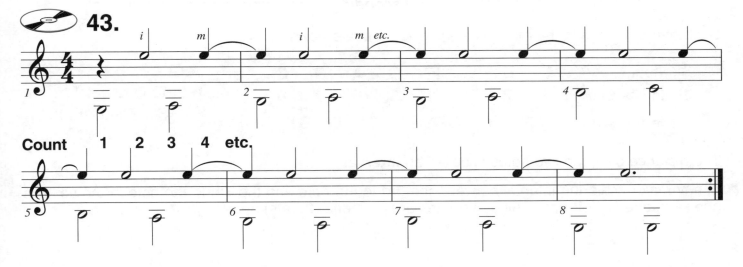

The Major Scale

The **major scale** is a series of **8** notes in alphabetical order that has the familiar sound:

Do   Re   Mi   Fa   So   La   Ti   Do

The **C major scale** contains the following notes.

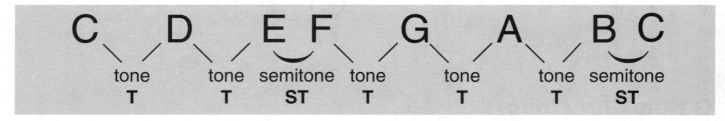

The distance between each note is two frets except for **EF** and **BC** where the distance is only one fret.

The distance of two frets is called a **tone**, indicated by **T**.

The distance of one fret is called a **semitone**, indicated by **ST**.

The Octave

An **octave** is the range of **8 notes** of a major scale. The first note and last note of a major scale always have the same name. In the **C major** scale the distance from the lowest C to the C note above it is one octave (8 notes).

The following example ascends and descends the C major scale.

 ## 44. The C Major Scale

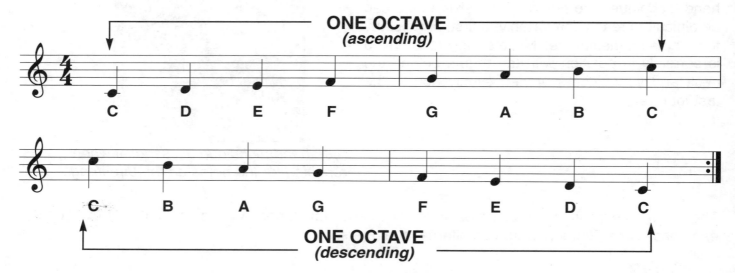

Each of the 8 notes in the major scale is given a **scale number**.

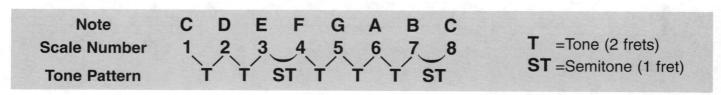

The distance between two notes is called an **interval**.

In any major scale the interval between the 3rd to 4th note and the 7th to 8th note in the scale is one semitone (1 fret) apart. All other notes are one tone (2 frets) apart.

Lesson 5

The Eighth Note

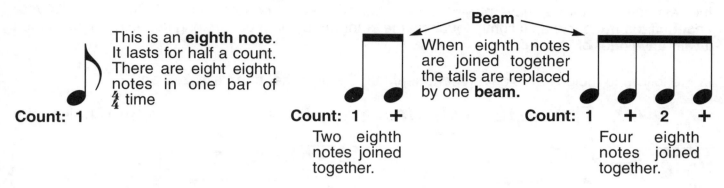

This is an **eighth note**. It lasts for half a count. There are eight eighth notes in one bar of 4/4 time

Count: 1

Beam

When eighth notes are joined together the tails are replaced by one **beam**.

Count: 1 +

Two eighth notes joined together.

Count: 1 + 2 +

Four eighth notes joined together.

45. How to Count Eighth Notes

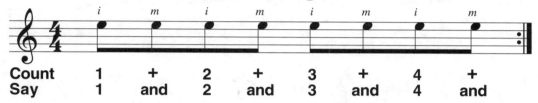

Count	1	+	2	+	3	+	4	+
Say	1	and	2	and	3	and	4	and

The following exercise combines eighth notes with other note values. Listen to the recording to hear the correct timing for this exercise.

46.

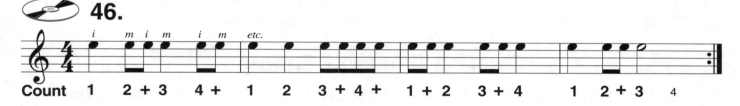

Count 1 2 + 3 4 + 1 2 3 + 4 + 1 + 2 3 + 4 1 2 + 3 4

You can now try some basic melodies that use the eighth note.

47. Skip To My Lou

Count 1 2 + 3 + 4 1 2 3 1 2 + 3 + 4 1 2 3

1 2 + 3 + 4 1 2 3 1 2 + 3 4 1 3

48. The Galway Piper

Count 1 2 3 4 1 2 3 + 4 + 1 2 3 4 1 2 3 + 4 +

1 2 3 4 1 2 3 4 1 + 2 + 3 + 4 + 1 2 3 4

The Eighth Rest

 This symbol is an **eighth rest**.
It indicates **half a beat** of silence.

If a rest comes after you have played a note, you must stop the note sounding. To do this, lift your finger off the fret but keep it lightly touching the string. To stop an open string sounding, lightly touch it with any finger of your left hand.

In the following melody an eighth rest appears on the first beat of bars 1, 3, 5 and 7.

49. The 1812 Overture
Peter Tchaikovsky

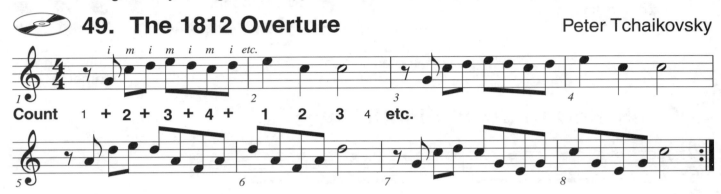

Count   1 + 2 + 3 + 4 +   1   2   3   4 **etc.**

The Lead-In

Sometimes a piece does not begin on the first beat of the bar. Any notes which come before the first full bar are called **lead-in notes** (or **pick-up notes**). When lead-in notes are used, the last bar is also incomplete. The notes in the lead-in and the notes in the last bar add up to one full bar. When you are playing chords do not strum until the first full bar, after the lead-in notes.

First and Second Endings

The next melody contains **first and second endings**. The first time you play through the song, play the first ending, (⌐1.   ¬), then go back to the beginning. The second time you play through the song, play the second ending (⌐2.   ¬) instead of the first.

First ending
⌐1.

Second ending
⌐2.

In the following melody **"The William Tell Overture"** play the first eight bars, then repeat from the beginning but don't play bar 8 the second time through, but instead go to bar 9.
This melody also begins on the fourth beat of a bar with two lead-in notes. This melody also has only three beats in the last bar because the last three beats the two lead-in notes at the beginning of the song add up to one complete bar (i.e. 4 beats)

50. The William Tell Overture
Gioacchino Rossini

Count 1 2 3 **4 +**   **1 2 + 3 4 + etc.**

Lesson 6

Sharp Signs

 This is a **sharp** sign.

A sharp sign written before a note on the staff means that you play the note that is **one fret higher** than the written note. Written below are two **F sharp (F♯)** notes.

When a sharp sign is written on the staff it is always written **before** the note.

F♯ Note *(1st string)*

The note on the second fret of the first string is an F♯ note. Use the second finger of your left hand to fret this note.

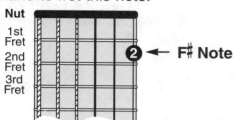

This F♯ note is notated on the staff as shown below.

F♯ Note *(4th string)*

The note on the fourth fret of the fourth string is also an F♯ note. Use the fourth finger of your left hand to fret this note.

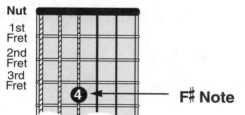

This F♯ note is notated on the staff as shown below.

The G Major Scale

The **G major** scale starts and ends on the note G and contains an F sharp (**F♯**) note. Written below are two octaves of the **G major** scale. Notice that the **G major** scale has the same patterns of tones and semitones as the **C major** scale. In a major scale the interval between the 3rd to 4th note and the 7th to 8th notes is a semitone (1 fret). In the **G major** scale, to keep this pattern of tones and semitones correct, an F♯ note must be used instead of an F note.

Note: Sometimes scales and single note melodies are played using the right hand fingers on the bass strings as well as the treble strings. Try the G major scale below using alternate *m* and *i* fingers.

51. The G Major Scale Over Two Octaves

Note	G	A	B	C	D	E	F♯	G		G	A	B	C	D	E	F♯	G
Scale Number	1	2	3	4	5	6	7	8	or	1	2	3	4	5	6	7	8
Tone Pattern		T	T	ST	T	T	T	ST			T	T	ST	T	T	T	ST

Key Signatures

The key of **C major** was discussed earlier. A piece of music that uses notes from the **C major** scale is said to be in the key of **C**. Similarly a piece of music that uses notes from the **G major** scale is said to be in the key of **G major**. Music in the key of **G** will contain F sharp (F#) notes.

Instead of writing a sharp sign before every F note on the staff, it is easier to write just one sharp sign after each clef. This means that all the F notes on the staff are played as F#, even though there is no sharp sign written before them. This is called a **key signature**.

C Major Key Signature

The **C major** scale contains no sharps or flats, therefore the key signature for the key of **C major** contains no sharps or flats.

G Major Key Signature

The **G major** scale contains one sharp, F#, therefore the key signature for the key of **G major** contains one sharp, F#.

Duets

It is important for you to play with other musicians and the best practice for this is the study of duets. Duets are written as two independent parts of music, which are indicated by Roman Numerals at the beginning of each line.
To get the most benefit from duets practice both parts.

The following duet is in the key of G. Remember to play all F notes as F sharp (F#)

52. Minuet in G

Johann Sebastian Bach

The Natural Sign

This is a natural sign.

A natural sign cancels the effect of a sharp or flat (see page 42) for the rest of that bar, or until another sharp or flat sign occurs within that bar. In the second bar of the following example a C# and D# are played. At the end of the same bar a D natural and C natural appear, cancelling the C# and D# sharp.

New Notes

Three new notes appear in the following duet.

C#
2nd String
2nd Fret
2nd Finger

D#
2nd String
4th Fret
4th Finger

F#
6th String
2nd Fret
2nd Finger

The next piece is in the key of E minor which is the relative key of G major and shares the same key signature. Relative Keys are discussed in detail on page 58.

53. Minuet in Em

Johann Sebastian Bach

Lesson 7

The Free Stroke

The free stroke is different to the rest stroke in that after striking a string the right hand finger does not rest on the next string but instead moves freely over that string. The free stroke produces a different sound to the rest stroke and is particularly used when each string needs to sustain rather than be dampened.

Position first finger to pick first string.

First finger moves across second string after picking first string

Try using the free stroke on the following exercise. Brace your right hand thumb on a bass string to help keep your right hand steady.

The cross above a note with a dotted line indicates that you should hold that note until the end of the dotted line.

 ### 54. Free Stroke Exercise

The next exercise combines free strokes on the first two strings with a simple bass line. Special attention should be given to the use of the right hand thumb on the third string (bars 2 and 3).
To get the correct effect for this exercise hold each bass note until the next bass note (2 beats). This effect can be heard clearly on the recording.

55.

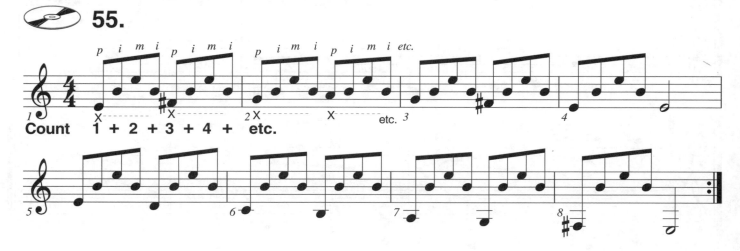

The next exercise is a simple Spanish guitar piece that features an open first string played repeatedly after every bass note. This is another example where the free stroke must be used. You will also notice that the thumb is used on the second string.

New Note

One new note appears in the following piece.

G#

**3rd String
1st Fret
1st Finger**

56. Malaguena

The next piece is a basic variation of a popular Classical piece by Isaac Albeniz. Use free strokes only. This piece also introduces $\frac{6}{4}$ time, a total of six beats to each bar.

57. Asturias

Chords

A chord is made up of three or more notes and is often played by holding down several notes at the same time with the left hand. Only the most common chords will be featured in this book. The first two chords to learn are the C Major, abbreviated to C and G Seventh, abbreviated to G7.

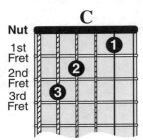

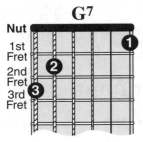

Arpeggios

Another right hand technique you will need to develop is arpeggio playing. Arpeggio playing is the individual picking of each note in a chord, normally played to a pattern. The free stroke is used to pick each note. The following exercise is an example of an arpeggio pattern played over a C major chord.

For this type of arpeggio pattern it is important to allocate a different finger for each treble string. The *i* finger for the third string, the *m* finger for the second string and the *a* finger for the first string. This will be the first time in this book the *a* finger on the right hand is used and may feel a little uncomfortable at first. Make sure your right hand is in the correct position so each string can be picked easily.

58.

Count   1   +   2   +   3   +   etc.

The next exercise applies an arpeggio pattern to both the C major and G Seventh chords.

59.

An example of an arpeggio pattern for 4/4 time is shown in the next example.

60.

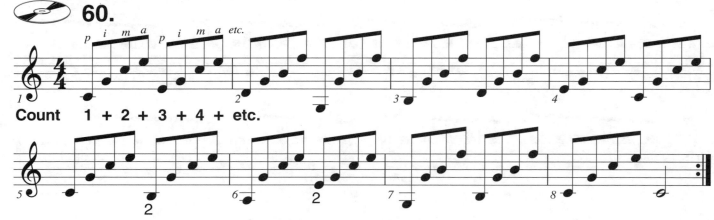

Count   1   +   2   +   3   +   4   +   etc.

Picking Two Notes Together

Another right hand technique you will need to develop is the picking of two notes together. This is another situation where the free stroke must be used. In the following example the *i* and *m* fingers play the first two strings at the same time. It is important to pick both strings as evenly as possible so each string has the same volume and tone.

61.

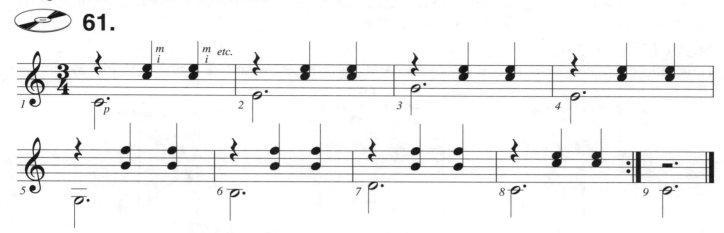

Picking Three Notes Together

It is also common practice to pick three strings together using the *i*, *m* and *a* fingers. As with picking two strings you will need to practice this until you have an even balance of volume and tone from all three strings.

62.

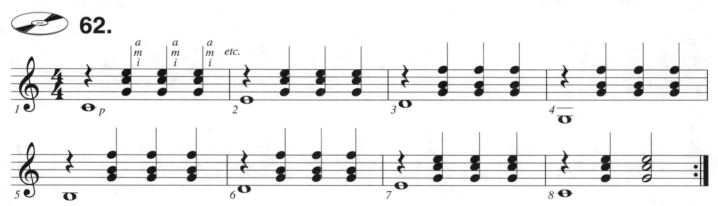

Picking Four Notes Together

Finally, the picking of three treble strings and a bass note simultaneously. The following exercise combines this technique with a $\frac{4}{4}$ time arpeggio pattern.

63.

Lesson 8

Classical Guitar Pieces

At this stage it will be possible to try your first full length Classical guitar piece. Waltz and Variation by Fernando Carulli uses all the techniques you have studied so far.

New Chords

Three new chord shapes appear in Waltz. The A Minor (Am), E Seventh (E7) and G Major (G).

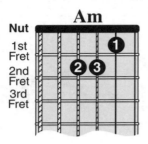

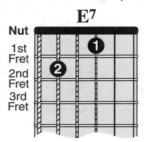

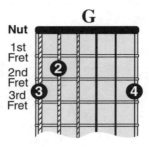

D.C. al Fine

Over bar 24, the instruction *D.C. al Fine* is written. This means that you play the song again from the beginning until you reach the word *Fine*.

64. Waltz

Ferdinand Carulli

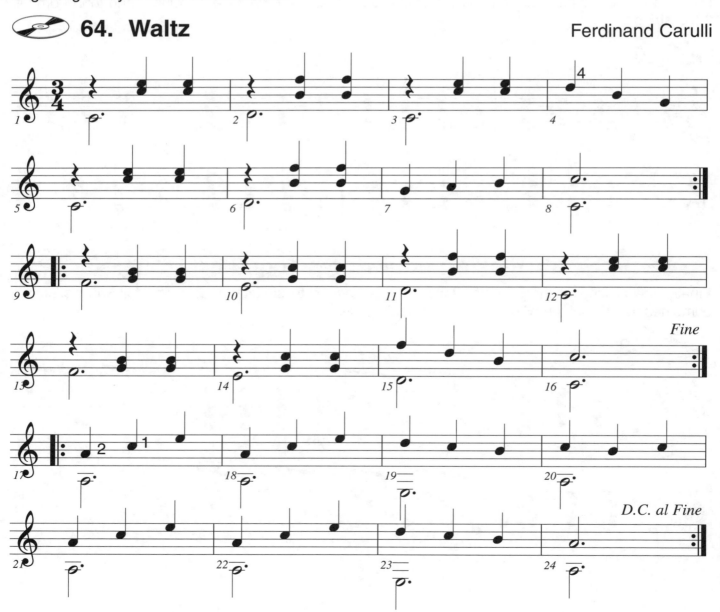

65. Waltz (Variation)

Ferdinand Carulli

The following pieces use notes and techniques studied throughout the book.

The first piece Andantino by Matteo Carcassi introduces $\frac{2}{4}$ time, two beats to each bar. Andantino is a common name for a music study that indicates the tempo of the piece. Andantino comes from another music term 'Andante' which means moderately slow. Andantino is slightly faster than Andante.

66. Andantino

Matteo Carcassi

The next study is also an Andantino but this time the composer is Mauro Giuliani. Special attention should be given to the left hand chord shape at the end of bar 14. This chord shape will prove to be difficult at first. Make sure you use the suggested fingers and your left hand is in the correct position.

67. Andantino

Mauro Giuliani

The following piece 'Waltz' by Ferdinand Carulli uses a strict arpeggio pattern.

68. Waltz

Ferdinand Carulli

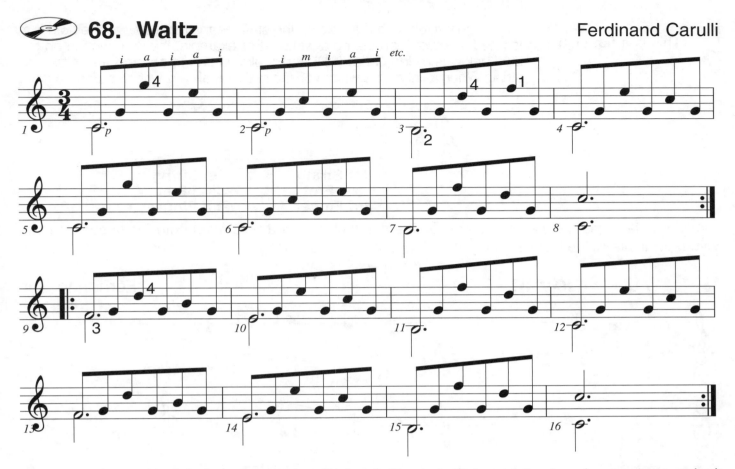

Study in A minor (Am) features a new note in bar 3. The note B (normally played as an open string) can also be played on the 3rd string, 4th fret. This enables you to fret the note B and D (2nd string, 3rd fret) at the same time.

Take care with the first shape in bar 6. Make sure you hold the F note (4th string, 3rd fret) for the duration of the first two beats of the bar.

The key of Am is the relative key of C major. Relative keys are discussed in detail on page 58.

69. Study in Am

Dionisio Aguado

Flat Signs

This is a **flat** sign.

A flat sign written before a note on the staff means that you play the note that is one fret lower than the note written. For example, the note written on the staff below is called **G flat** (**G♭**), and is played on the **second** fret of the **1st** string. When a flat sign is written on the staff, it is always written **before** a note.

1st String
3rd Fret
3rd Finger

1st String
2nd Fret
2nd Finger

Study in C features a G flat. Try to play all the notes clearly and hold each note for its correct time value, particularly the F note on the 4th string, 4th fret, as highlighted in the music.

70. Study in C

Fernando Sor

Lesson 9

The Dotted Quarter Note

A dot written after a quarter note means that you hold the note for **one and a half** beats.

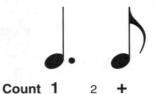

Count **1** 2 +

A dotted quarter note is often followed by an eighth note.

Try the following exercise which uses the dotted quarter note. Special attention should be given to the count below the music. Listen to the recording to hear the correct timing.

71. Dotted Quarter Note Exercise

Count   **1**   2 **+ 3**   **1**   2 **+ 3**   **1**   2 **+ 3**   **1**   2   3

1   2 **+ 3**   **1**   2 **+ 3**   **1**   2 **+ 3**   **1**   2   3

The dotted quarter note is featured in the following piece by Karl Beyer.

72. Andante

Karl Beyer

Count   **1**   2 **+ 3** etc.

A Note *(1st string)*

The note on the fifth fret of the first string is an A note. Use the fourth finger of your left hand to fret this note.

This A note is written on the first leger line above the staff.

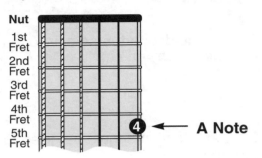

A Note

The A note on the first string is introduced in the following pieces.

In the first piece, the D# note on the 2nd string must not ring at the same time as the open 1st string (E). After playing the D# lift the left hand finger of the string at the same time as the E note is played.

73. Study

74. Minuet

Robert de Visée

The Six Eight Time Signature

6/8 This is the **six eight** time signature.
There are six eighth notes in one bar of 6/8 time. The six eighth notes are divided into two groups of three.

Count: 1 2 3 4 5 6   or   1 2 3 4 5 6

When playing 6/8 time there are **two** beats within each bar with each beat being a **dotted quarter note.** (This is different to 4/4 and 3/4 time where each beat is a quarter note). **Accent** (play louder) the 1 and 4 count to help establish the two beats per bar.

Try the following exercise which is in 6/8 time. Special attention should be given to the count below the music. Listen to the recording to hear the correct timing.

75.

76. Barcarolle

M. Carcassi

The Eighth Note Triplet

Eighth note **triplets** are a group of **three** evenly spaced notes played within one beat. Eighth note triplets are indicated by three eighth notes grouped together by a bracket (or a curved line) and the number *3* written either above or below the group.

Count: 1 + a
Say: one and ah

The eighth note triplets are played with a third of a beat each. **Accent** (play louder) the first note of each triplet group as it will help you keep time.

The triplet is introduced in the following example. Listen to the recording to hear the correct timing.

77. Triplet Study

M. Carcassi

Count 1 + ah 2 + ah 3 + ah 4 + ah etc.

The next piece is in 2/4 time, only two quarter notes to each bar. The triplet is used for the second half of the piece.

78. Allegretto

M. Giuliani

Lesson 10

New Notes

There are four more notes you will need to know on the first string, the notes B (7th fret), C (8th fret), D (10th fret) and E (12th fret).

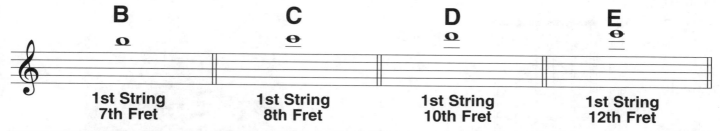

B	**C**	**D**	**E**
1st String 7th Fret	1st String 8th Fret	1st String 10th Fret	1st String 12th Fret

The Half Bar

A half bar is when the first finger of your left hand frets the first three strings at the same time. In the following piece a half bar is used on the 5th fret in the 5th and 9th bars of the music. To finger a half bar correctly ensure your left hand thumb is behind the neck and your first finger is almost straight, as shown in the photo. Study the diagram below. A bar is indicated on a diagram by a thick line.

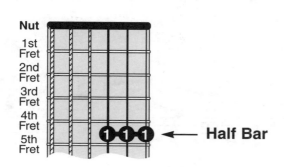

The Half Bar

The notes you will be holding are the notes C on the 3rd string (same note as the C on the 1st fret of the 2nd string), E on the 2nd string (same note as the open 1st string) and the A note on the 1st string. The symbol ½CV above the music means half bar at the 5th fret, C indicates bar and V (Roman numeral) indicates 5. Sometimes a bracket is also added to the notation to indicate a bar.

79. Half Bar Study

The Full Bar

A full bar is when the 1st finger of your left hand frets all six strings at the same time. In the following piece a full bar is used on the 1st fret in the 13th bar of the music. To finger a bar correctly ensure your left hand thumb is behind the neck and your first finger is straight, inline with the fretwire, as shown in the photo.

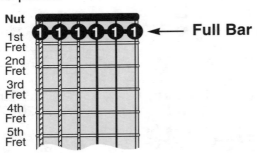

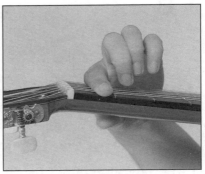

The Full Bar

The following exercise is in $\frac{12}{8}$ time, a total of 12 eighth notes to a bar.

The symbol CI indicates a full bar at the first fret, C indicating bar, I (Roman numeral) indicating 1.

Note: In bars 10 and 14 a half bar is used. In both cases only the 1st and 2nd strings are barred.

80. Study in C Major

Francisco Tarrega

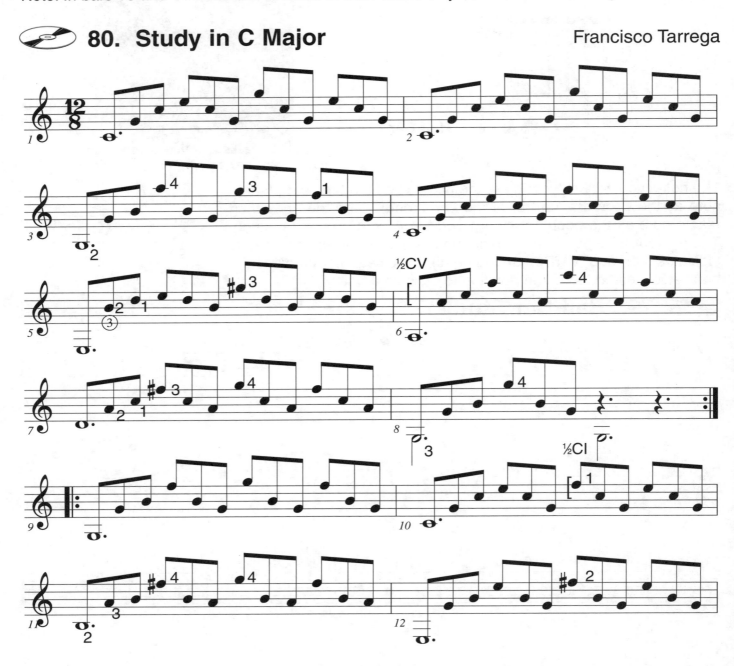

New Chords

Two new chord shapes appear in the following piece. The F Major (F) and C Seventh (C7).

Dynamics

Dynamics are the varying degrees of softness and loudness that can be applied to passage of music. The most common dynamic indicators are shown below. These symbols will appear below a music staff and will apply to all music notes from that point in the music until the next dynamic symbol appears.

p (piano) = soft

pp (pianissimo) = very soft

mp (mezzo piano) = moderately soft

f (forte) = loud

ff (fortissimo) = very loud

mf (mezzo forte) = moderately loud

A new note also appears in the following piece, the note **B♭** on the 3rd string, 3rd fret.

81. Allegro

Anton Diabelli

The Sixteenth Note

This is a **sixteenth note**. Its value is one quarter of a beat. There are sixteen sixteenth notes in one bar of $\frac{4}{4}$ time

Count: 1

Beam

When sixteenth notes are joined together the tails are replaced by two beams.

Count: 1 e

Two sixteenth notes joined together.

Count: 1 e + a

Four sixteenth notes joined together.

82. Sixteenth Note Study

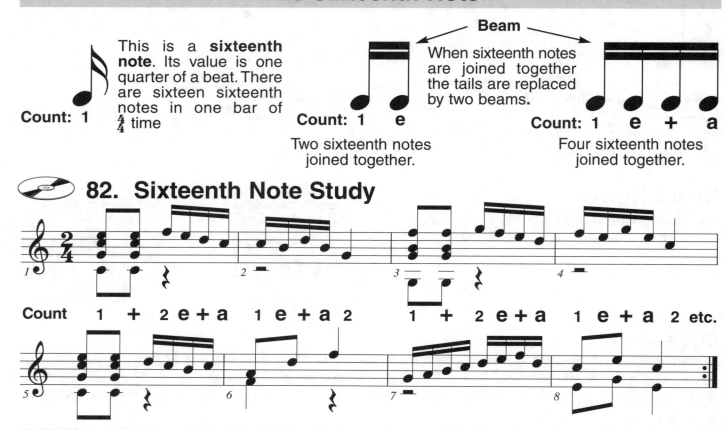

Count   1 + 2 e + a   1 e + a 2   1 + 2 e + a   1 e + a 2 etc.

The Sixteenth Rest

This symbol is a **sixteenth rest**. It indicates **quarter a beat** of silence.

83. Study in A Minor

Mauro Giuliani

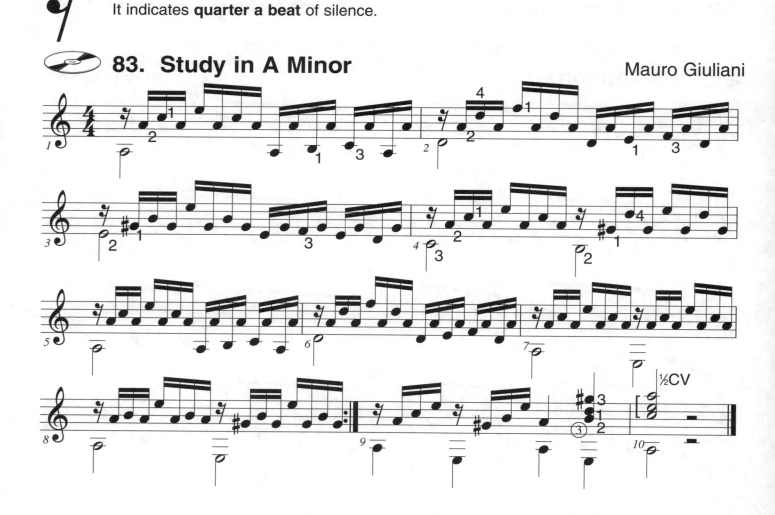

Using the Rest and Free Stroke Together

There are many pieces that require the use of the rest and free stroke. This situation often occurs when there is a melody on the 1st and 2nd strings played over an arpeggio pattern. The following examples uses a rest stroke on the first string and free strokes on the 2nd and 3rd strings.

84. Rest and Free Stroke Study

85. Study in E Minor

Francisco Tarrega

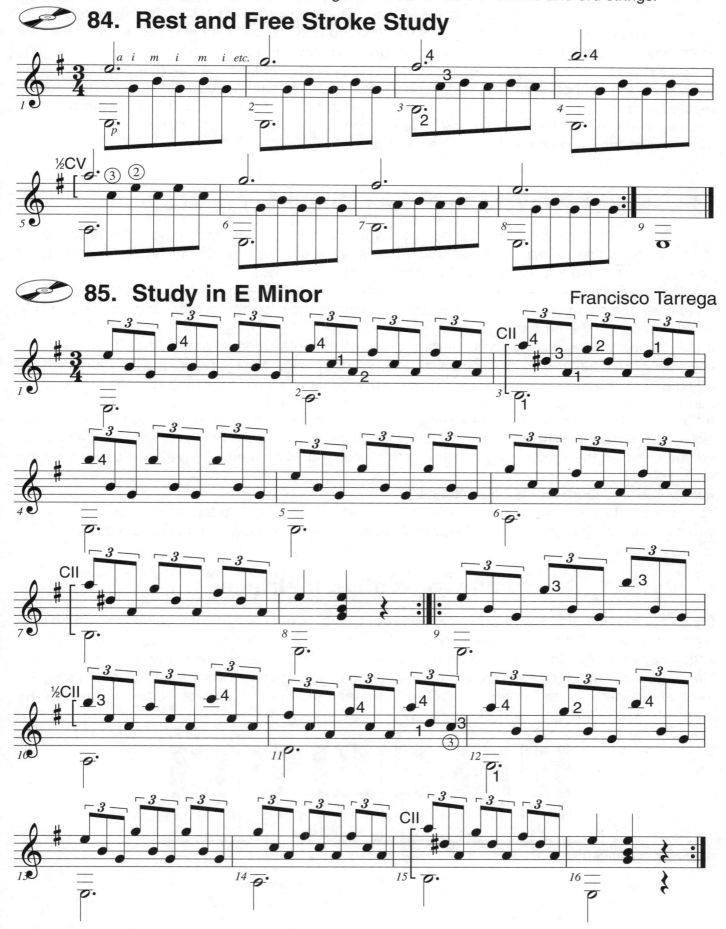

How to Tune Your Guitar

Before you commence each lesson or a practice session you must tune your guitar. If your guitar is out of tune everything you play will sound incorrect even though you are holding the correct notes. If you want to play along with the CD your guitar must be tuned to 'concert pitch'. This is a standard tuning that all musicians tune to so that they can play 'in concert' with each other. It is possible for a guitar to be in tune with itself (e.g. you strum a chord and it sounds in tune) but out of tune with a piano which would be tuned to concert pitch. Outlined below are the methods you can use to tune to concert pitch i.e. electronic tuner, tuning to another instrument, tuning fork and pitch pipes. Also discussed is a method of tuning all guitarists must know i.e. tuning the guitar to itself. This tuning method is essential to know because when tuning to concert pitch you may only be given one note (usually the open 5th string A) so you have to know how to tune the other strings to this note. To tune your guitar using an electronic tuner (see page 6).

How to Tune Your Guitar to the CD

At the beginning of the recording, the six open strings of the guitar are played. You should tune each string of your guitar to each of these notes. These notes are the same pitch as an electronic tuner so if you have tuned to an electronic tuner your guitar will be in tune with the CD.

The first note played is the open 6th string (E note).

If the open 6th string on your guitar sounds the same as the note on the recording, your string is **in tune**. Proceed to the next string.

If the note on the recording sounds **higher**, it means your 6th string (E note) is **flat**. Turn the tuning key slowly in a counter-clockwise direction. This will raise the pitch of your string. Play your 6th string again and compare it with the recording. Keep doing this until your 6th string (E note) sounds the same as the recording. Usually you will not have to turn the tuning key very far.

If the note on the recording sounds **lower**, it means your 6th string is **sharp**. Turn the tuning key slowly in a clockwise direction. This will lower the pitch of your string. Play your 6th string again and compare it with the recording. Keep doing this until your 6th string (E note) is the same as the recording.

Follow this procedure for the other strings.

To check if your guitar is in tune strum a chord. Most students find it easier to tune up to a note, so you may wish to detune your string to slightly below the recording, and tune up from there.

Tuning to Another Instrument

If you are playing along with another instrument, it is essential that your guitar be in tune with that instrument. Tune the open strings of your guitar to the corresponding notes of the accompanying instrument. E.g. to tune to a piano, tune the open 6th string to the E note on the piano, as shown on the keyboard diagram. Then tune your guitar to itself from this note using the method outlined on the following page, or tune each string of your guitar to those notes of the piano shown on the keyboard diagram.

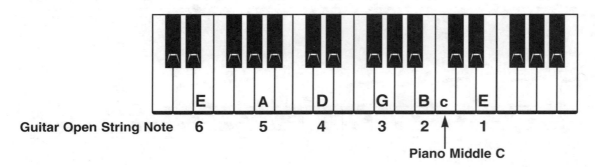

Tuning Fork

Tuning Fork

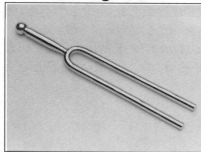

A tuning fork produces a note (usually the 5th string A Note) which you tune one string to. Then you tune the other strings to that string.

Pitch Pipes

Pitch Pipes

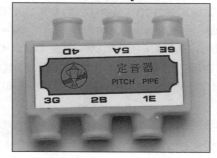

Pitch pipes produce notes that correspond to each of the six open strings.

Tuning the Guitar to Itself

Unless you are using an electronic tuner, to be able to tune the guitar accurately usually requires many months of practice. You will probably need your music teacher or musician friend to help you tune when you are learning.

If you do not have another instrument to tune to, you can tune the guitar to itself by using the following method.

1. Place a left hand finger on the **6th** string (thickest string) at the the **fifth** fret, and play the string.
2. Play the **open 5th string** (an **A** note). If this note sounds the same as the note you played on the **6th** string at the **fifth** fret, the **A** note is **in tune**.
3. If the open A string sounds **higher**, it means that it is **sharp**. Turn the tuning key slowly in a clockwise direction. This will lower the pitch of the string. Play the two strings again and compare the notes. Keep doing this until the open A string sounds the same as the E string at the fifth fret.
4. If the open A string sounds **lower**, it means that it is **flat**. Turn the tuning key slowly in a counter-clockwise direction. This will raise the pitch of the string. Play the two strings again and compare the notes. Keep doing this until the open A string sounds the same as the E string at the fifth fret.
5. Tune the **open 4th string** (a **D** note), to the note on the **fifth** fret of the **5th** string, using the method outlined above.
6. Tune all the other strings in the same way, except for the **open 2nd string** (a **B** note), which is tuned to the note produced on the **fourth** fret of the **3rd** string. (See diagram).
7. To check the tuning, strum a chord.

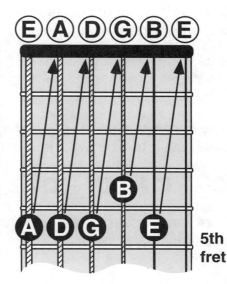

Tuning Hints

One of the easiest ways to practice tuning is to actually start with the guitar in tune and then de-tune one string. When you do this, always take the string **down** in pitch (i.e.loosen it) as it is easier to tune 'up' to a given note rather than 'down' to it. As an example slightly detune the 4th string (D). If you play a chord now, the guitar will sound out of tune, even though only one string has been altered (so remember that if your guitar is out of tune it may only be one string at fault).

Following the correct method, you must tune the open 4th string against the D note at the fifth fret of the 5th string. Play the note loudly, and listen carefully to the sound produced. This will help you retain the correct pitch in your mind when tuning the next string.

Now that you have listened carefully to the note that you want, the D string must be tuned to it. Play the D string, and turn its tuning key at the same time, and you will hear the pitch of the string change (it will become higher as the tuning key tightens the string). It is important to follow this procedure, so that you hear the sound of the string at all times, as it tightens. You should also constantly refer back to the correct sound that is required (i.e. the D note on the fifth fret of the 5th string).

Scales

A scale can be defined as a series of notes, in alphabetical order, going from any given note to its octave and based upon some form of set pattern. The pattern upon which most scales are based involves a set sequence of **tones** and/or **semitones**. On the guitar, a tone is two frets and a semitone is one fret. As an example, the **B** note is a tone higher than **A**, (two frets), whereas the **C** note is only a semitone higher than **B** (one fret). Of the other natural notes in music, **E** and **F** are a semitone apart, and all the others are a tone apart.

Natural Notes

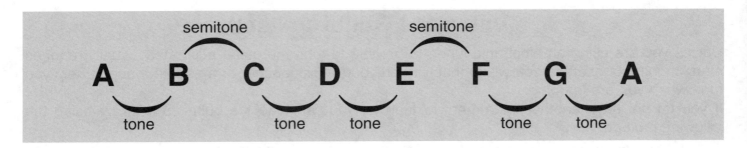

In music theory, a tone may be referred to as a **step** and a semitone as a **half-step**.

The main types of scales that you need to become familiar with are the **chromatic**, **major**, **minor** and **minor pentatonic** scales.

The Chromatic Scale

The **chromatic** scale is based upon a sequence of **semitones** only and this includes every possible note within one octave. Here is the **C chromatic scale**.

C C♯ D D♯ E F F♯ G G♯ A A♯ B C

The same scale could be written out using flats, however it is more common to do this when descending, as such;

C B B♭ A A♭ G G♭ F E E♭ D D♭ C

Because each chromatic scale contains every possible note within one octave, once you have learnt one you have basically learnt them all. As an example, the **A** chromatic scale (written below) contains exactly the same notes as the **C** chromatic scale, the only difference between them being the note upon which they commence. This starting note, in all scales, is referred to as the **tonic** or **key note**.

The A Chromatic Scale

A A♯ B C C♯ D D♯ E F F♯ G G♯ A

The Major Scale

The most common scale in Western music is called the **major scale**. This scale is based upon a sequence of both tones and semitones, and is sometimes referred to as a **diatonic** scale. Here is the major scale sequence;

TONE	TONE	SEMITONE	TONE	TONE	TONE	SEMITONE
T	T	S	T	T	T	S

Starting on the **C** note and following through this sequence gives the **C major** scale;

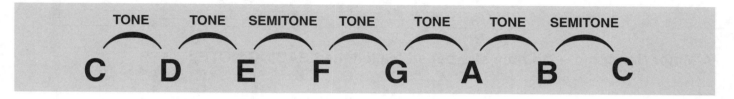

and in musical notation.

Roman numerals are used to number each note of the major scale. Thus **F** is the **fourth** note of the **C major** scale, **G** is the **fifth**, and so on.
The major scale will always give the familiar sound of **DO, RE, MI, FA, SO, LA, TI, DO**.

The major scale **always** uses the same sequence of tones and semitones, no matter what note is used as the tonic. The table below list the 13 most commonly used major scales.

In order to maintain the correct sequence of tones and semitones, all major scales except **C major** involve the use of either sharps or flats. You will notice, when playing these scales, that they all maintain the familiar sound of **DO, RE, MI, FA SO, LA, TI, DO**.

	T	T	S	T	T	T	S
C MAJOR	C	D	E	F	G	A	B	C
G MAJOR	G	A	B	C	D	E	F♯	G
D MAJOR	D	E	F♯	G	A	B	C♯	D
A MAJOR	A	B	C♯	D	E	F♯	G♯	A
E MAJOR	E	F♯	G♯	A	B	C♯	D♯	E
B MAJOR	B	C♯	D♯	E	F♯	G♯	A♯	B
F♯ MAJOR	F♯	G♯	A♯	B	C♯	D♯	E♯	F♯
F MAJOR	F	G	A	B♭	C	D	E	F
B♭ MAJOR	B♭	C	D	E♭	F	G	A	B♭
E♭ MAJOR	E♭	F	G	A♭	B♭	C	D	E♭
A♭ MAJOR	A♭	B♭	C	D♭	E♭	F	G	A♭
D♭ MAJOR	D♭	E♭	F	G♭	A♭	B♭	C	D♭
G♭ MAJOR	G♭	A♭	B♭	C♭	D♭	E♭	F	G♭
Roman Numerals	I	II	III	IV	V	VI	VII	VIII

The Minor Scale

In western music there are three different minor scales. These are the **pure minor**, the **harmonic minor** and the **melodic minor**. Each features a slightly different sequence of tones and semitones, as illustrated in the examples below using **A** as the tonic.

A Minor 'Pure' Scale

A Minor Harmonic – 7th note sharpened (called the LEADING NOTE):

A Minor Melodic – 6th and 7th notes sharpened when ascending and returned to natural when descending.

Of these three minor scales outlined above, the **melodic minor** is the most commonly used. The table below lists the 13 most commonly used minor scales.

	T	S	T	T	T	S	T	T	S	T	T	S	T		
A MELODIC MINOR	A	B	C	D	E	F#	G#	A	G♮	F♮	E	D	C	B	A
E MELODIC MINOR	E	F#	G	A	B	C#	D#	E	D♮	C♮	B	A	G	F#	E
B MELODIC MINOR	B	C#	D	E	F#	G#	A#	B	A♮	G♮	F#	E	D	C#	B
F# MELODIC MINOR	F#	G#	A	B	C#	D#	E#	F#	E♮	D♮	C#	B	A	G#	F#
C# MELODIC MINOR	C#	D#	E	F#	G#	A#	B#	C#	B♮	A♮	G#	F#	E	D#	C#
G# MELODIC MINOR	G#	A#	B	C#	D#	E#	G	G#	F#	E♮	D#	C#	B	A#	G#
D# MELODIC MINOR	D#	E#	F#	G#	A#	B#	D	D#	C#	B♮	A#	G#	F#	E#	D#
D MELODIC MINOR	D	E	F	G	A	B♮	C#	D	C♮	B♭	A	G	F	E	D
G MELODIC MINOR	G	A	B♭	C	D	E♮	F#	G	F♮	E♭	D	C	B♭	A	G
C MELODIC MINOR	C	D	E♭	F	G	A♮	B♮	C	B♭	A♭	G	F	E♭	D	C
F MELODIC MINOR	F	G	A♭	B♭	C	D♮	E♮	F	E♭	D♭	C	B♭	A♭	G	F
B♭ MELODIC MINOR	B♭	C	D♭	E♭	F	G♮	A♮	B	A♭	G♭	F	E♭	D♭	C	B♭
E♭ MELODIC MINOR	E♭	F	G♭	A♭	B♭	C♮	D♮	E♭	D♭	C♭	B♭	A♭	G♭	F♭	E♭

Keys and Key Signatures

When music is talked of as being in a particular key, it means that the melody is based upon notes of the major scale (or minor scale) with the same name e.g. in the **key of C**, **C major** scale notes (i.e. **C, D, E, F, G, A** and **B**) will occur more frequently than notes that do not belong to the **C** scale (i.e. sharpened and flattened notes).

In the **key of G**, **G** scale notes will be most common (i.e. the notes **G, A, B, C, D, E** and **F♯** will occur frequently). You will notice here that **F♯** occurs rather than F natural. However, rather than add a sharp to every **F** note, an easier method is used whereby a sharp sign is placed on the **F** line (the top one) of the staff at the beginning of each line. This is referred to as the **key signature**: thus the key signature of **G major** is **F♯**.

Written below are the key signatures for all major scales so far discussed.

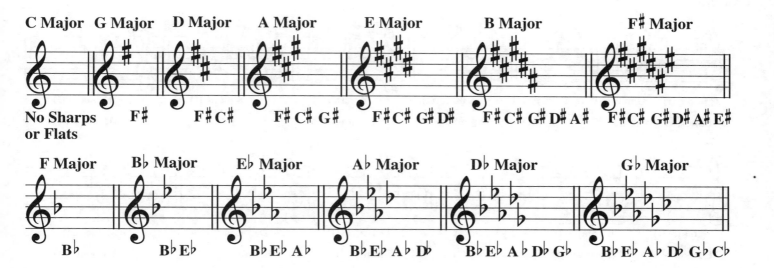

It can be seen, then, that each key signature is a shorthand representation of the scale, showing only the sharps or flats which occur in that scale. Where an additional sharp or flat occurs, it is not included as part of the key signature, but is written in the music, e.g. in the **key of G**, if a **D♯** note occurs, the sharp sign will be written immediately before the **D** note, **not** at the beginning of the line as part of the key signature.

Relative Keys

if you compare the **A minor** "pure" minor scale with the **C major** scale you will notice that they contain the same notes (except starting on a different note). Because of this, these two scales are referred to as "relatives"; **A minor** is the relative minor of **C major** and vice versa.

Major Scale: C Major

Relative Minor Scale: A Minor (pure)

The harmonic and melodic minor scale variations are also relatives of the same major scale, e.g. **A harmonic** and **A melodic minor** are relatives of **C major**.

For every major scale (and ever major chord) there is a relative minor scale which is based upon the **6th note** of the major scale. This is outlined in the table below.

MAJOR KEY (I)	C	Db	D	Eb	E	F	F#	Gb	G	Ab	A	Bb	B
RELATIVE MINOR KEY (VI)	Am	Bbm	Bm	Cm	C#m	Dm	D#m	Ebm	Em	Fm	F#m	Gm	G#m

Both the major and the relative minor share the same key signature, as illustrated in the examples below:

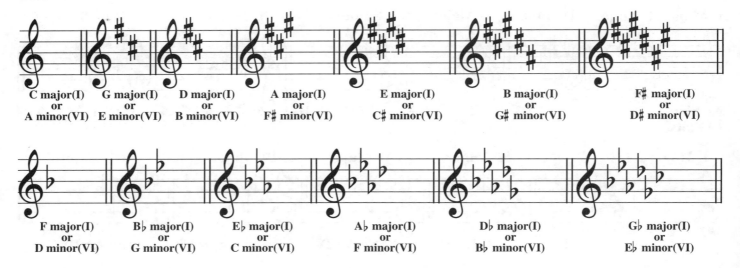

The sharpened **7th** note that occurs in the relative minor key is never included as part of the key signature. Because each major and relative minor share the same key signature, you will need to know how to distinguish between the two keys. For example, if given a piece with the key signature of **F#** thus:

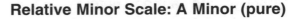

It could indicate either the **key of G major** or its relative, **E minor**. The most accurate way of determining the key is to look through the melody for the sharpened **7th** note of the **E minor** scale (**D#**). The presence of this note will indicate the minor key. If the **7th** note is present, but not sharpened, then the key is more likely to be the relative major (i.e. **D natural** notes would suggest the **key of G major**).

Another method is to look at the first and last chords of the progression. These chords usually (but not always) indicate the key of the piece. If the piece starts and/or finishes with **Em** chords then the key is more likely to be **E minor**.

Glossary of Musical Terms

Accidental — a sign used to show a temporary change in pitch of a note (i.e. sharp ♯, flat ♭, double sharp ✗, double flat ♭♭, or natural ♮). The sharps or flats in a key signature are not regarded as accidentals.

Ad lib — to be played at the performer's own discretion.

Allegretto — moderately fast.

Allegro — fast and lively.

Andante — an easy walking pace.

Arpeggio — the playing of a chord in single note fashion.

Bar — a division of music occurring between two bar lines (also called a 'measure').

Bar chord — a chord played with one finger lying across all six strings on the guitar.

Bar line — a vertical line drawn across the staff dividing the music into equal sections called bars.

Bass — the lower regions of pitch in general. On guitar, the 4th, 5th and 6th strings.

Chord — a combination of three or more different notes played together.

Chord progression — a series of chords played as a musical unit (e.g. as in a song).

Clef — a sign placed at the beginning of each staff of music which fixes the location of a particular note on the staff, and hence the location of all other notes.

Coda — an ending section of music, signified by the sign ⊕ .

Common time — and indication of $\frac{4}{4}$ time — four quarter note beats per bar (also indicated by 𝄴).

D.C al fine — a repeat from the sign (indicated thus 𝄋) to the word 'fine'.

Dynamics — the varying degrees of softness (indicated by the term 'piano') and loudness (indicated by the term 'forte') in music.

Eighth note — a note with the value of half a beat in $\frac{4}{4}$ time, indicated thus ♪ (also called a quaver).

The eighth note rest — indicating half a beat of silence is written: ♪

Enharmonic — describes the difference in notation, but not in pitch, of two notes.

Fermata — a sign, ⌢ , used to indicate that a note or chord is held to the player's own discretion (also called a 'pause sign').

Flat — a sign, (♭)used to lower the pitch of a note by one semitone.

Forte — loud. Indicated by the sign 𝆑 .

Half note — a note with the value of two beats in $\frac{4}{4}$ time, indicated thus: 𝅗𝅥 (also called a minim). The half note rest, indicating two beats of silence, is written: ▬ on the third staff line.

Harmony — the simultaneous sounding of two or more different notes.

Interval — the distance between any two notes of different pitches.

Key — describes the notes used in a composition in regards to the major or minor scale from which they are taken; e.g. a piece 'in the key of C major' describes the melody, chords, etc., as predominantly consisting of the notes, **C, D, E, F, G, A,** and **B** — i.e. from the **C** scale.

Key signature — a sign, placed at the beginning of each stave of music, directly after the clef, to indicate the key of a piece. The sign consists of a certain number of sharps or flats, which represent the sharps or flats found in the scale of the piece's key.

Leger lines — small horizontal lines upon which notes are written when their pitch is either above or below the range of the staff.

Legato — smoothly, well connected.

Major scale — a series of eight notes in alphabetical order based on the interval sequence tone - tone - semitone - tone - tone - tone - semitone, giving the familiar sound **do re mi fa so la ti do**.

Melody — a group of notes of varying pitch and duration, and having a recognizable musical shape.

Metronome — a device which indicates the number of beats per minute, and which can be adjusted in accordance to the desired tempo.

the desired tempo.

Moderato — at a moderate pace. **Natural** — a sign (♮)used to cancel out the effect of a sharp or flat. The word is also used to describe the notes **A, B, C, D, E, F** and **G**; e.g. 'the natural notes'.

Note — a single sound with a given pitch and duration.

Octave — the distance between any given note with a set frequency, and another note with exactly double that frequency. Both notes will have the same letter name.

Open voicing — a chord that has the notes spread out between both hands.

Pitch — the sound produced by a note, determined by the frequency of the string vibrations. The pitch relates to a note being referred to as 'high' or 'low'.

Plectrum — a small object (often of a triangular shape)made of plastic which is used to pick or strum the strings of a guitar.

Position — a term used to describe the location of the left hand on the guitar fret board. The left hand position is determined by the fret location of the first finger. The 1st position refers to the 1st to 4th frets. The 3rd position refers to the 3rd to 6th frets and so on.

Quarter note — a note with the value of one beat in $\frac{4}{4}$ time, indicated thus ♩ (also called a crotchet). The quarter note rest, indicating one beat of silence, is written: 𝄽 .

Repeat signs — used to indicate a repeat of a section of music, by means of two dots placed before a double bar line.

Rhythm — notes grouped into patterns that can be measured against a beat.

Semitone — the smallest interval used in conventional music. On guitar, it is a distance of one fret.

Sharp — a sign (♯) used to raise the pitch of a note by one semitone.

Staccato — to play short and detached. Indicated by a dot placed above the note.

Staff — five parallel lines together with four spaces, upon which music is written.

Syncopation — the placing of an accent on a normally unaccented beat.

Tempo — the speed of a piece.

Tie — a curved line joining two or more notes of the same pitch, where the second note(s) is not played, but its time value is added to that of the first note.

Timbre — a quality which distinguishes a note produced on one instrument from the same note produced on any other instrument (also called 'tone colour'). A given note on the guitar will sound different (and therefore distinguishable) from the same pitched note on piano, violin, flute etc. There is usually also a difference in timbre from one guitar to another.

Time signature — a sign at the beginning of a piece which indicates, by means of figures, the number of beats per bar (top figure), and the type of note receiving one beat (bottom figure).

Tone — a distance of two frets; i.e. the equivalent of two semitones.

Transposition — the process of changing music from one key to another.

Treble — the upper regions of pitch in general.

Treble clef — a sign placed at the beginning of the staff to fix the pitch of the notes placed on it. The treble clef (also called 'G clef') is placed so that the second line indicates as G note.